Getting Over a Broken Heart

JUNE LAUREL OWEN, PSY.D.

Red Penguin
BOOKS

Getting Over a Broken Heart

Copyright © 2024 by June Laurel Owen, Psy.D.

All rights reserved.

Published by Red Penguin Books

Bellerose Village, New York

Library of Congress Control Number: 2023922006

ISBN

Softcover   978-1-63777-505-9

Digital   978-1-63777-504-2

For Jean Owen who, although my therapist for more than twenty years, has been so much more. At so many critical points in my life she has been so many different things to me: a parent, friend, mentor, the voice of reason and sanity during insane times and, above all, a warm, caring and empathic woman who truly understands without judgment. Without her, this book would not have been written. The type of steady, unwavering and healing connection I have had with her is what I wish for everyone who has suffered a broken heart.

For my daughter, Laurel Jean Owen, who has given my life a new purpose and meaning. Above all, she has brought a joy and depth of love that has brightened my life during many heartbreaking times. Laurel's middle name is in honor of Jean Owen.

Contents

Acknowledgments

I want to thank my good friend, Carol Purdy who has helped with my manuscript from the very beginning. I put it aside as other life events took my attention and got back to it on an intermittent basis. Every step of the way, she read it and gave me valuable feedback which has shaped its final form.

Even though she is no longer with us, I thank my mom, Dorothy Greene Owen who was an avid supporter of my writings. She always loved poetry and, in her youth, collected poems by anonymous authors which she clipped out of her local papers. She gave them to me before she died and most of the epitaphs in my book are from her clippings. She is sorely missed and I wish she were here to read my completed book.

Introduction

This book is inspired, not just by my work as a clinical psychologist dealing with clients who have suffered terrible heartbreaks, but by my own personal experiences and those of friends. I will be talking about my own relationships as well as those of my clients and others with whom I am close. Names and identifying information are changed but the stories are authentic.

The impetus for this book was a relationship breakup that was especially painful for various reasons. I call him Alex and he appears in different sections.

In Part One, I describe the experience of a broken heart and some of the forces such as loss, the blow to one's self and the death of hope that feed this terrible pain.

In Part Two, The Searching Heart, I focus on relationships that are dysfunctional or, for whatever reason, not meant to be. I describe how we get into them and what makes it so difficult to break away once we are aware of the heartache they cause.

In Part Three, I talk of the ways in which we heal and move on. I close with two case histories that highlight many of the key points in the first two parts and describe how one can work through such heartbreak and establish a stronger, happier self.

PART ONE

The Broken Heart

The night has a thousand eyes
The day but one
But the light of a whole world dies
When day is done

The mind has a thousand eyes
The heart but one
But the light of a whole life dies
When love is done

~Anonymous

Love, whether it be the love of a mate, a child or any significant being in one's life is one of the most enlivening experiences one can have. Losing it can feel as though a part of yourself has died. That is why we hold onto it, even when it is against all odds.

In this part, I will describe some of the things that cause this pain which include loss, the blow to one's self and the death of hope.

CHAPTER I

THE PAIN OF LOSS

My spirit flew in feathers then
That is so heavy now
No summer pool can ever cool
The fever on my brow

~Thomas Hood

To fly so high, to feel such joy, only to have it come crashing down; that is the pain of being in love and having it end. When you lose a loved one through any means, there is a devastating feeling of loss. There may be profound feelings of sadness, emptiness, depression, hurt, anger, desperation and panic as though a part of yourself has been ripped away forever.

Yet, each loss has its own unique characteristics. Loss through a breakup differs from loss through death or suicide although the pain may be no less intense.

Also, each person has their own unique life experience which shapes how the loss will be felt.

The first person I will talk about is Pat. She had a series of very unusual and traumatic life experiences which determined how she responded to heartbreak. I have begun with her because she so clearly illustrates the shattering pain of loss and the conflict within herself that made it difficult for her to move on.

While not everyone has such a dramatic story, we all have our own unique experiences and all are equally valid and important.

---

1. Loss through a breakup

> "It was like my heart was made of glass and someone took it to the top of the Empire State Building and dropped it to the ground and it shattered into a million pieces … I feel like Humpty Dumpty … broken into a million pieces and no one can put me back together again."

Pat, a passionate woman who sucked the juices out of life, spoke these words as she lay in her hospital bed, telling me the story of a particularly devastating heartbreak.

She had an unusual beauty that shone from within and without. Soft brown curls framed her sculpted face with its sensual features. She had a hearty laugh and a wild humor. Her natural ability to listen and respond with unbridled empathy and warmth won the hearts of many men.

Pat met Mark in a hospital where she had undergone an amputation. Diabetes had robbed not just her sight, but toes on her left foot. She was fingering her rosary beads and praying out loud when she heard an unfamiliar voice.

"Your prayers are answered! I'm here now." Mark was a neurosurgeon who tended to Pat's roommate. Pat laughed. He took her hand and said, "I want you to touch it," placing her hand over the now empty place where her toes had been. She would never forget this gesture. She knew that, to him, she was beautiful and whole.

He was immediately enchanted by Pat. After she left the hospital, she returned to her tiny apartment. He would visit often, take her out for romantic dinners and ask about her dreams. She said she wanted a home with a large, sunny room where she could feel the warmth of the sun caressing her.

He replied that he wanted to buy a house and set up her dream room with its sunny window. They spent many hours indulging in this fantasy. After a short, whirlwind romance, he asked her to marry him.

Pat was afraid. Her ex-husband had left her for another woman as soon as she became ill. Despite this heartbreak, she became engaged to another man who later died of cancer. The thought of yet another heartbreak was more than she could stand. It was hard for her to admit, even to herself, the intensity of her love for Mark. A wall had gone up and she was afraid to let it down. And so she resisted his marriage proposal.

Months went by. One day, as she was cleaning her bathtub, she heard the phone ring. It was Mark. They hadn't spoken in a while and so she had involved herself in an obsessive cleaning spree as though to wash away her feelings.

"I got married," he said. Pat was silent.

She felt sick. As she put it, her heart was shattered into a million pieces and she didn't know how to put it back together again.

Such pain comes and goes in waves. There is a moment of respite and then the wave hits, like a tidal wave and all the feelings come back again full force.

Years went by. Pat suffered many more physical and emotional losses. She lost her leg to gangrene and underwent numerous surgeries. Other suitors came and went. Eventually, she wound up in a nursing home. But as she sat in her hospital bed and relayed her story to me, she would always go back to thoughts of Mark. *Had she made a mistake?* she would ask herself. *If I married him, I might not be here but sitting in that sunny room in my own home with Mark.*

Brief though that relationship was, it had filled her with joy at one time. It was so hard for her to come to terms with the fact that such happiness had ended.

With such relationship breakups, there is the compulsion to go over and over it again, as though in doing so, you might magically undo the past. Pat would forever, until her death, be plagued with a shadow of a doubt about her decision.

Although Pat's story is devastating, there is hope within this darkness. Despite her many severe physical challenges, the fact that she lost her sight and limb, she was beautiful and whole to Mark and other suitors who later came along. It is also a powerful statement about the critical role of self-worth when dealing with heartbreak and loss and this will be addressed in more depth later on.

2. Loss through death

"But O for the touch of a vanished hand,
And the sound of a voice that is still!"

~Tennyson

No words better describe the pain of losing one forever. When you have lost a loved one through death, there isn't a sense of "what did I do wrong?" Yes, sometimes you wonder if you could have done more for your loved one, perhaps obtained more medical help or been more supportive. But for the most part, this is not at the forefront. The one thing most people say is, "I can't get over the permanence." When my father died, my mother said, in disbelief, "He'll never walk through that door again."

The mind cannot truly grasp this. It is so hard to reconcile being with nonbeing. A truly religious person can sometimes keep their mate alive through the belief that they have moved onto another plane. There is something to hold onto, although the pain may be no less intense. But when you do not have such solid beliefs, the feelings can be very confusing. You want to maintain the connection but are not sure how.

For everyone, there is the feeling of being left. For someone with a history of abandonment, old traumas are reawakened.

When you lose your loved one through a breakup, the mind may work and rework everything. "How did it happen ... what did I do ... where did things go wrong ... what did I fail to see?" At the back of your mind is the hope that, perhaps some day, things will work out and you can be together again down the road. At any rate, there is the illusion of hope, no matter how unrealistic, because that other person is still alive.

When the person has died, there can be no such hope and this brings its own special type of agony.

---

3. Jim

I lost Jim twice, once through a breakup and once through death. What distinguished these? The first time it was a personal blow that shattered my self-esteem. There was a sense of desperation because I felt I had lost a part of myself and I did not know how to get it back. I knew I just felt empty, dead and totally disconnected from life.

I met Jim at college. He was working on his doctorate in psychology, and I was working on my masters. The first time we connected was on an elevator at school after class. He looked right into my eyes, which did not see too well even then.

I was slowly losing my eyesight but could get around and read to some degree. As I walked back to my dorm, my blind cane self-consciously tucked under my arm, he skipped along. He was tall and big boned, with a rough hewn Irish look; reddish brown hair, hazel eyes, ruddy complexion and an elfish, whimsical way about him, despite his size. He had a devilish chuckle and a sort of country hick way of talking. I found him enchanting.

We arranged for a study date. The study date consisted of many books strewn on the floor and the two of us laughing and cuddling on my daybed in my tiny dorm room.

I fell in love. Thanksgiving was joyous. I looked forward to Christmas with romantic exhilaration. We spent most of Christmas week together. That is when I saw subtle signs that things weren't quite right. Actually they seemed subtle at the time but, in retrospect, they now seem more obvious.

I remember throwing my arms around him on New Year's Eve and saying, "You're such a sweetie." He stood stiffly and said, in a voice I couldn't quite read except to say that it had a somewhat ominous ring to it, replied "You think so?" I saw his level of dysfunction; the filthy apartment he lived in, the habit of sleeping all day and the general chaos that surrounded him. I later found out that he was on probation at school for his dysfunctional behavior. But I thought I could change all this, and make it right if I just tried hard enough.

I remember a disturbing dream that seemed to foretell what would happen. I was at my parents' house, trying to use their wall phone to get help; somehow I wanted to get through to Jim but the wire sizzled and frayed into so many scorched pieces. Something did not feel right.

Yet, when the phone call that tore me apart came, it was a total shock. He called a couple of days after New Year's and said that we should talk about our relationship. I felt the knot in my stomach and my arms began to stiffen as though to brace for the blow. He said, "I care about you a whole lot but I'm not in love with you." He then went on to say that he wanted to get married and have a family and couldn't see doing it with a woman who was losing her eyesight. He reminisced over a past relationship and how much he loved this other woman, that she had a three year old and they felt like a little family. As he put it, "All systems go."

I put down the phone, ran to the bathroom and threw up. I was completely traumatized; it was as though I were hit in the stomach with a baseball bat. The rest of the night was torture. It seemed that every loss, every blow had come crashing down on me all at once. I was sick. I felt like I was going crazy. I needed someone to talk to immediately and so I took a cab to the nearest emergency room where I talked to a sympathetic psychiatrist for more than an hour. I was in a severe depression for many weeks.

In retrospect, I can see that part of the devastation was the blow to my self-esteem. I was just informed that he did not love me and that I would not make an adequate parent because of my eyesight.

Many years later, I would experience a very different kind of loss.

After this terrible breakup, Jim called a year later and we eventually established a friendship. In fact, he became one of my closest friends for more than 15 years. He was the one person I could call any time of day or night and share my feelings, including new heartbreaks.

He told me that he had a new found respect for me when, three weeks after the breakup I confronted him with my remark that many blind couples raised children. Ironically, he spent the next 15 years trying to re-establish what we once had but I knew this was not possible. Our relationship was forever tinged with a note of longing and anguish.

I sometimes found myself caught up in his fantasies of marriage and children. When I decided to have a baby on my own, since my biological clock was running out and there was no suitable mate in sight, I toyed with the notion of him being the father. Logic took over and I turned to a sperm bank instead. When I thought I was pregnant, I called him up and he sang Tu ra lu ra lu ra to me and told me to kiss my stomach. I can still hear his voice singing the little Irish lullaby to me. It was the last time I would hear his voice.

Once again, a phone call came that would tear me apart, but in a very different way. I came home from work one day and my father was sitting in a chair. He slowly said, "Jon McDevitt called." This was Jim's brother who lived in Michigan and I knew there could be only one reason for his call. Yet I asked, "What did he call about?" as though he were calling to tell me some news on the radio. The words "Jim died" hit me like a lightning bolt in much the same way as the first time. I had been trying to call him for several days but did not get through. He had been lying in his bed, his hands cupped over his stomach and his wire rimmed glasses in place on top of the big dome that would never again rise and fall.

I lost him, but somehow the feelings were different.

The funeral drove all the feelings home. As his brothers entered the church carrying the oak casket an Irish tenor sang Cat Steven's *Morning has Broken* in a quavering voice. I choked back tears, not wanting to break down so soon. But as the brother he loved so much passed my pew, he touched my arm and spoke softly. I burst out crying. I could hear John's muffled tears.

At the grave site I stroked the oak casket. I couldn't believe that he was in there. Once again, a broken heart, but so different from the first time. There was no crushing blow to the self, just a feeling of total loss and a yearning to touch him just one more time. There was not that incredible anxiety, desperation and blow to my self-esteem. I truly grieved. I was filled with irrational thoughts and fantasies. I imagined that this was all a terrible mistake, that he was really alive and the lid to the casket would fly open and reveal a live Jim. For a brief moment, I had a wild fantasy that a doctor could somehow extract sperm and I could have a baby from Jim. I wanted to hold onto him, to keep the bond alive, to keep Jim alive forever through a baby that was half him.

4. Grief versus depression

People often use terms such as grief, depression and sadness interchangeably although they are quite different.

The depression into which I fell after my breakup with Jim was caused by a crushing blow to my sense of self which left me feeling dead, empty and disconnected from life. Thus, in many ways, depression is a much more intolerable state than that of grief.

There is no worse state than being disconnected from oneself, others and the world in general. Most religions and healing arts emphasize that we are all connected, all part of a greater whole. Depression is the antithesis of this idea. It is as though we died but are still walking around in an empty shell of a body.

When I try to describe depression, I sometimes think of the H.G. Wells story *The Time Machine*. The part I think of is when the main character fast forwards to a time when all life on Earth is gone following a nuclear war. The sun was starting to nova. It was dim and the Earth was parched and cold. The only life form was a monstrous crab, a sort of cosmic monster that mutated from radioactivity. The picture was one of total desolation.

Lara, a woman whom I will describe later on, said that, each time a particular relationship seemed to have ended, "It felt like I was the sole survivor of an earthquake."

Grief is so different from the kind of torment we go through when a dysfunctional relationship ends.

With grief, you are connected to your feelings. You may feel connected to your loved one. When Jim died, I did not feel the same blow to my sense of self that I felt when we broke up. I felt a connection to him and a desire to keep him alive through any means, no matter how irrational. The feeling was one of sadness and loss, not desperation and deadness.

In many ways, depression is a much more intolerable state because it is a state of emotional disconnection.

Although depression and grief are distinct states, both can occur as the result of a relationship breakup or death and you can alternate between them.

To further complicate the picture, depression can also serve a protective function. Protective in the sense that it deadens feelings and shields you from overwhelming sadness and pain. However, in the long run, it is a poor solution since it pulls you away from your real feelings and ultimately causes you to feel even more disconnected and lonely.

5. Loss through suicide

Karen was engaged to a man who adored her. He was sensitive, but full of anxiety and overwhelmed by any disruption in the relationship. He would become very clingy, causing her to seek space for herself, which would cause him to panic. They talked and talked every time there was the slightest problem between them. But nothing seemed to alleviate his anxiety. She would become overwhelmed and back off, causing him to pursue her even more frantically.

Despite their rocky relationship, they dreamed of the beautiful life they would build together. He filled her with visions of the dream house and children they would have, the family vacations, barbecues, trips to the beach, etc. However, he could not control his underlying panic and desperation. He was terrified she would leave him, even though there was no real reason to think this.

They had spent a lovely day together, filled with affection, lovemaking and shared fantasies over a great meal.

As the fateful day progressed, the inevitable disruptions came. He felt she was ignoring him when she wanted to socialize with friends at the nightclub that topped the evening. She felt overwhelmed and in need of some space. She decided to drop him off and go home in order to regroup. He begged her not to go. She assured him that she loved him and would call him as soon as she got home. True to her word, she called.

After a few moments on the phone, she heard a gunshot. She raced over to his house and found him dead on the floor. She could not forgive herself for not heeding his plea of "Don't leave me." While she understood that she was not truly responsible for his death and that it would have probably happened anyway, it was hard for her to get over the "what if's."

She questioned herself over and over. "Was I selfish? Would he still be alive if I didn't leave him that night?"

Although she knew that the suicide had more to do with him and his unresolved feelings given his history of abandonment, she still played the last hours over and over in her mind like a tape, searching for answers, answers she had but they never felt like enough.

She wondered, in the back of her mind, "what if" she had not left that day. Also, how could she buy the notion that it was not about her when he shot himself in the head while on the phone with her?

When you lose your mate through suicide, the mixture of emotions is very complex. In some ways it combines some facets of the first two types of loss. As with a breakup, your mate has deliberately left you. Also, you work and re-work everything in an effort to gain some sense of control. As with the death of a loved one, the loss is permanent.

However, suicide has its own unique characteristics. Two of the most pronounced feelings are guilt and shame. Guilt for feeling that perhaps you did not see the signals or maybe failed to act on signals you saw. Shame for feeling that you have fallen short, that you have betrayed your loved one because, "after all, if only I had seen the signs, he might not have killed himself."

One of the hardest things to grasp is that the suicide is not about you, yet it might be directed at you. When Karen's fiancé shot himself, the bullet not only pierced his brain, it pierced her heart, forever leaving emotional scars.

6. Traumatic states

The loss or impending loss of a relationship can be very traumatic. The definition of trauma is something that is out of one's usual experience. It is a sudden intrusion of something that is so overwhelming it cannot be processed. We may play the tape over and over in our minds. When we lose someone, through death or a breakup, we go over and over it, yet it sometimes seems to no avail. There is a temporary relief as you talk about it with an understanding person. But when you hang up that phone or that door closes, you are once again alone with your thoughts and feelings.

Jerry, a shy but friendly man with an infectious laugh, fell into a state of severe anxiety and depression following a traumatic event. Two days after Christmas he found out that his wife of ten years was having an affair.

He was completely traumatized and was plagued by intrusive thoughts of the other man. He was in a state of acute anguish and sobbed uncontrollably to the point where he could no longer breathe. He barely slept and would wake up at 4 a.m. each morning in a panic. He said that as he fell asleep, the full impact would hit him and one time he woke up screaming.

We practiced some meditative techniques designed to anchor his mind at such times. In his second session, he said he felt better, that he practiced the meditation techniques and found that if he suddenly opened his eyes as soon as the obsessive thoughts arrived upon awakening, he felt better. However, after a few weeks, his severe anxiety gave way to depression.

He eventually moved out of his house on the pretext of sorting things out with his wife. He started to have occasional moments when he felt better, but they were quite fleeting. He continued to have intrusive thoughts of the other man, which he tried to push out of his mind. In describing the intrusive thoughts and feelings, he marveled at how suddenly they would appear. That is the nature of trauma. It appears suddenly and without warning, making it difficult to process.

Most people don't really understand the nature of trauma. They associate it with very dramatic events such as rape, the diagnosis of a catastrophic illness or some other devastating event. A trauma can be so much more subtle.

Trauma can be the experience of a loved one being there for you emotionally, connecting with you and then suddenly withdrawing. We all suffer from trauma, whether obvious or subtle, at some time in our lives. We just don't recognize it as such.

My own therapist first made me truly understand the nature of traumatic states. She knew I suffered from them to a marked degree but I did not. I only knew that, I experienced overwhelming feelings of panic at times and they always seemed to be within the context of a relationship.

I first became aware that I suffered traumatic states when I was in a relationship with Jack. There would be some sudden disruption in the relationship that would trigger a state of alarm. My heart would pound and I would sometimes experience dramatic changes in my body temperature. Usually, I would get ice cold. Then I would immerse myself in a hot bath for an hour or more, but the effect would be only temporary. The only thing that would help would be to fix the disruption.

When this relationship finally ended, I felt devastated. I didn't even cry when he told me he thought we should go our separate ways. I was numb. I slept little that night and the next day I woke up and felt sick, sick at heart. I cried every day for two weeks. Mornings seemed particularly tough since the trauma would hit me full force.

I was inconsolable. Nothing anyone could say or do seemed to relieve the pain. I remember what one of my old loves once said, "It's like the only person who can fix it is the person who caused it in the first place."

CHAPTER II
BLOW TO ONE'S SELF

What feeds this terrible pain; why does it hurt so much? Yes, there is the pain of the loss, but there is often so much more. This is most obvious in relationship breakups that don't seem so deserving of such torment.

When I look back on most of my relationships and those of my friends and clients, the one thing that stands out as feeding the intense pain and sense of loss is the blow to the self. It is as though a part of you has been torn away.

We lose a part of ourselves in a relationship. This is the price of intimacy.

We all experience some blow to the self when a relationship ends because of the fact that, in any close relationship, the other person has become a part of our daily experience, our world, our self. But for some, because of their life experiences, the blow can be especially devastating.

In these instances, there is a pile up of injuries to the self, an accumulation of losses and traumas that weaken one's sense of self, making it especially hard to endure yet another blow.

1. The pile up

Nina was an attractive, slim, personable and fun loving woman who fell into a severe depression after the breakup with a man who tormented her in many ways. He drank, was a womanizer and criticized any of her physical imperfections, whether real or imagined. Because of a particular physical anomaly, she felt insecure about her ability to attract a decent man. He played on this insecurity and tore down her sense of self till there was almost nothing left but an empty shell of depression.

She contemplated plastic surgery, despite the fact that most others thought she was quite pretty. However, she was ambivalent about this since she did not want to feel that she was doing it just for him, but for her own self. A stronger part of her felt that, if someone truly cared about her, they would accept her as is. Every time she broke loose from him he maneuvered his way back into her life. He would show up at her doorstep with roses and presents and seduced her with empty promises. This was hard for her to resist since she felt so rejected and lonely and craved the attention.

But the fact remained that he was poisonous for her. She was miserable most of the time. In analyzing her depression, it was clear that the main, if not sole contributor was the blow to her sense of self; not just one blow, but repeated ones that had the cumulative effect of diminishing her strength.

These repeated blows were piled on top of a self that was already undermined by an abusive ex-husband as well as abusive parents.

Each loss not only has its unique characteristics, causing its own special brand of pain as you recall the tender moments, it often seems that every loss you ever had as well as every crushing blow to yourself is in there with it.

Every time Nina's boyfriend rejected her, she would relive not just the pain of his previous rejections but the rejection by her parents in childhood as well as that of her ex-husband.

When your sense of self has been undermined since childhood by parents and other significant people, as was the case with Nina, this will lay the shaky ground upon which future losses will be experienced.

2. The one who leaves

So far, in looking at relationship losses, the focus has been on the one left behind. When you are the one being rejected, the blow to yourself can be crushing. In essence, you feel "kicked to the curb." Some say, "I feel like I've been thrown out like a piece of garbage." The case of Nina dramatically exemplifies this feeling.

However, the pain can be just as great for the person leaving. Some people overly empathize with the person they are leaving. They can step into that person's shoes but have trouble getting back into their own.

Veronica was unhappily married for years. Her husband drank and cheated on her. She wanted to leave but felt unable, not because of money or competence but because of guilt and shame, mainly shame. This dilemma was further compounded when he became disabled from a stroke. He went into a rehabilitation center for many months where he suffered more strokes and further disability. She had already been his caretaker and it was clear that, if he came home, this servitude would be a life sentence. She realized that the only chance she stood was to leave the relationship while he was away, a thought that horrified her. However, she knew that, if he came home, she would become paralyzed and unable to end the marriage. Thus, after working through many turbulent feelings, she informed the rehab agency that she wanted to get a divorce. However, she remained faithful as a friend, visiting him regularly.

In her mind, it would have been easier if he had left her for another woman as opposed to leaving him herself. Here, the sense of self was involved, but in a very different way. She did not have to contend with the crushing blow of being "kicked to the curb." However, she had to endure another torment. She felt that she was a bad person for leaving a man when he was at his lowest. She felt that she was, as she put it, "a disgrace." After all, who could leave a handicapped mate?

It took a great deal of self-reflection and strength for her to work through these feelings. Indeed, she could only too easily imagine what it would be like to be stricken with a devastating ailment and then left. Regaining her sense of self-worth was a challenge that took some time, but it was a challenge she won.

Cara was a self-confident woman who unknowingly entered into a relationship with a man who had an addiction problem. Since he carefully concealed this problem, she did not know about it until she was very entrenched with him. It was clear that he cared for her a great deal and undoubtedly hid this problem in order to protect the relationship. However, this strategy backfired. Because he had hidden such a major thing from her for a considerable time, her trust was shaken and she did not know how to get it back. She loved him very much but was terrified of living a life as a prisoner to someone's addiction and of forever harboring feelings of distrust. No matter how much she tried to work through these feelings, there was always a shadow of a doubt. She decided to end the relationship. She became depressed and went through many of the same feelings one might go through if left behind. She hoped for the phone call and became more depressed when it didn't come. She went over and over the conflicts in her mind, searching for answers. Was he telling the truth? Was it true that he wasn't concealing anything else? Was he cheating? Did he truly love her? If so, why didn't he fight for the relationship? Did he ever love her or was that a lie and so on and so forth. She wanted answers, she wanted control over an uncontrollable thing. She went through the same sort of obsessive questioning and angst that one goes through when left behind.

CHAPTER III

THE DEATH OF HOPE

Hope is a thing with feathers that perches in the soul

~Emily Dickinson

Another thing that adds to the terrible pain is the death of hope. When you lose someone, you don't just lose them as a person; you lose all the hopes, dreams and fantasies about the future that are woven into the relationship.

Alex came to symbolize everything I ever hoped for in a relationship. He seemed to embody all of my wishes, dreams and desires. He seemed tuned in, responsive and we had so much in common. We loved animals, nature and children. Both of us were very sad that we had missed out on having a family. At my late age, I had been certain that no man would want to start a family, let alone get totally excited about it. But, when he found out that I was trying to adopt a baby, he was thrilled. Both of our minds raced with excitement as we tried to envision a beautiful future. I couldn't believe that I still had a shot at the whole American dream of love, marriage and children. I had been attempting to have a child on my own but, after meeting him, I realized once more that I truly wanted the whole package.

When the relationship fell apart, I didn't just lose Alex. I lost the whole dream, a dream I had my entire life but had buried only to be reawakened by him.

CHAPTER IV

THE NEED FOR AN ANSWER

When you go through a breakup, how often do you ask yourself "why?" You wait for the letter, the email, for the phone to ring, anything to regain that connection and to also find out why, as though there is something you can do about it. I cannot say how many times I have heard either myself, a client or a friend say, "if only I knew why," as though in knowing, the pain would be less. We need that fantasy that, somehow in knowing, we have control over a situation that we really can't control. It is especially hard to accept when a relationship ends without any closure. The person may just stop calling or say they want to end it without any explanation.

One of my first relationships was with Eddie. It was a passionate, adolescent romance. It felt magical. However, he left without any explanation or warning although, in retrospect, there were signs. I called his house but he screened my calls until, one day, he answered the phone and said, "I have nothing to say to you at this time." I questioned and questioned him; "Does that mean ever or just now ... what happened ... why ..." He repeated his initial response in a cold voice. I wondered why; I wanted to talk, to understand, to get a handle on it.

One morning I heard a noise in the garage which was right next to my bedroom. I ran downstairs, but before I could get to the front door, my parents told me that Eddie had run into the garage, left something and then ran back to his car and took off at top speed. We went into the garage and found the giant painting I had given to him as a gift many months earlier. I examined the painting closely. First, I looked at the back of it, running my hand over every inch, feeling desperately for the note I was sure he must have attached. Nothing. Over and over again I looked at the back of the painting, thinking that maybe he had written a little message in pencil. I so hoped to see the words "love Eddie" or "give me a call" or, most of all, "I love you." Again, nothing. Days passed and I repeated this act, knowing full well that nothing would be there. It was as though some message would magically appear. It was like the way you might inspect a letter over and over, looking for more, the hidden truth.

---

1. The phone call that never comes

The anxiety of waiting for that phone call after a breakup is indescribable. Every time you hear that ring, your heart races. Since I am now blind, I have a talking caller ID and wait for the numbers to be announced. If the first number matches the one I'm dying to hear, my heart pounds as I stop dead in my tracks, waiting, with shaking hands to grab the phone. Although this only takes place in less than a second, it feels like an hour and the after effects drain my body. How many of us have gone through this, in some form or another? You begin to simultaneously hope for and dread that ring. Hope for that magical reconnection, dread that it will make you feel even worse. After all, you may have gained a little distance and don't want to lose any ground.

---

2. To call or not to call, that is the question

Most can relate to the internal struggle over whether or not to call, particularly when there is no closure.

As I noted earlier, Alex seemed to embody all my greatest dreams and desires. We went on a dream vacation together but the dream began to unravel towards the end of it. When we returned home, I saw him only once. Before the next time we were supposed to get together he called and said, "You're not going to like what I have to say...I don't think we'll be getting together this weekend." He said he was under a lot of pressure, his blood pressure was at an all time high and he was having a meltdown. I remarked that a part of it must have to do with me and he reluctantly said that it might be a little part but that he was going through a lot, that he had important life decisions to make and needed the time to himself. He said he was confused and didn't know what he was thinking or feeling and would I do him a favor and not ask him any questions. I reluctantly obliged. He said he would call me over the weekend. He never did. Somehow, I knew he would not call me Saturday, that he would wait for the last minute and call me Sunday night, if at all.

The phone call never came. The weekend was nightmarish. I did not stay home, but I did fanatically check home for messages. When the machine announced that there were new messages, my hope and dread would rise. I cursed every message that was not from him. By Tuesday, I agonized over whether or not to call. I asked the opinion of others and got as many opinions as there were people. One said that her pride would get in the way, that she would not want the other person to know they were so important. Another said she would call and be casual. Another advised that I call and say, "Call me within 24 hours...if you don't, I will consider this relationship over." Still another was ready to take me to his house and confront him outright.

I went back and forth a million times in my mind, seriously considering each piece of advice. There were the pros; it is good to take action. As I tell clients, it is one of the greatest antidepressants. Also, being in a waiting, passive mode is utterly destructive to your sense of self. Then there were the cons; the biggest one being, what if he said what I did not want to hear? Also, what if I got his answering machine, left a message since he always screened calls and he didn't call me back? Then I would be a total wreck every time the phone rang.

On Thursday, I decided to call. I felt empowered by my decision. However, when I went to pick up the phone I broke into a vicious sweat. A friend was with me and told me I should just wing it, that I couldn't rehearse what I wanted to say. I dialed. His machine picked up and I hung up.

A month went by with still no call. I was plagued with the notion of how to deal with his machine and guarantee a call back. I decided I would leave a casual message. It said, "Hi, this is June, how are you? I just wanted to ask you something, so just call me back tonight or tomorrow morning before noon." I gave a time frame so as to put limits on the amount of emotional torture to which I would be subjected while waiting for the call. My tone was light and breezy, belying my inner state of chaos. The next day his number was announced on my talking caller ID. I was stunned. I didn't pick up right away since I wasn't fully prepared; I had just walked in the door. Also, I felt a tinge of indignation. *Why should I pick up the minute he decides to call? Let me call at my leisure and convenience even though I hadn't experienced anything resembling these states in a long time.*

When I called back, he picked up. Unknown to him, I recorded his end of the conversation so I could go over it after we hung up. In a calm, reserved voice full of pride, I gave my little speech with my perfectly timed questions. I told him that the last time we spoke he asked for space. I said, "I honored that and have given you a month." I said, "I think that you, I, and the relationship were deserving of some closure, a face to face contact, and at the very least a phone call." I said, "If you didn't want the relationship and we both have our reasons (letting him know I rejected him as well; my pride couldn't stand for less), the least you could have done is call."

He agreed in a nervous voice. It was good to hear his anxiety. There is nothing worse than to feel that someone has had the capacity to crush you and that you have had virtually no effect on them, that they have moved on, perhaps to another relationship. It is the ultimate blow to your self-esteem.

If I had to do it over again, I would have called much sooner. Also, I would have been true to my feelings, a concept I will go into in much more depth in Part Three.

Ironically, one year later he called and left a message saying, "I know this is probably a foolish question, but would you like to go out for Indian food some time?" I never called him back.

PART TWO

The Searching Heart

❧

Who has known heights and depths shall not again know peace
Not as the calm heart knows

~Anonymous

There is no greater high than falling in love. Waves of euphoria sweep over you. Your head is in the clouds. Blissful fantasies consume your every thought. You feel alive. Life is exciting and the simplest things bring joy. And so the heart will forever search for such love since it knows the joy that it brings. When it feels this love slipping away through any means, it struggles to hold on because the fall from such heights is so painful.

In this part, I will look at the various ways in which one gets into a love relationship and holds on, even when it is doomed.

CHAPTER I
THAT DEADLY CHEMISTRY

One of the key things that drives us into relationships in the first place is chemistry. Everyone knows what it is but virtually no one knows how to define it. We just know when it does or doesn't exist. Many say, "It just clicks." Some define it as sexual attraction. While this is a part of it, it is not, as most of us know, the whole picture. Although it is difficult to give a precise definition, it is possible to describe some of the facets that comprise it.

First, there is the blending of needs and personalities.

1. The press of needs

The need that is most pressing is the one that will first surface in a relationship. Indeed, it is what gets us into most relationships to begin with. It is also the source of many problems since it often blinds us to the other person. A prospective mate who is totally inappropriate for us may intuit our needs which causes us to become seduced into a relationship that is bad for us. Thus, you may become attached to the wrong person since they offer the promise of filling that need.

If you are starved for affection, the need for physical contact may take over and lure you into a relationship that is essentially bad for you. But, unfortunately, you become attached before you really have a chance to size up the situation. A very pressing need has a way of taking over. You so want to meet that need, you begin to think short range pleasure as opposed to long range gain.

---

2. Repeating history

There is another component of chemistry that is quite tricky. In order for there to be that chemistry, there has to be some familiarity. By this I mean there is something about that person that is connected to your past. Most have heard of the notion that we "marry our mother" or "marry our father." We often are attracted to people who either have characteristics of our family of origin, whether good or bad, or play out some conflict or mode of interaction that is familiar.

Candice was derailed by the death of her mother. They did everything together and had an intense bond that seemed as though it would go on forever. Her mother was loving but needy, and had many quirks, not the least of which were a hypercritical streak and a need to control every aspect of her daughter's life. Years after her mother's death, she became involved with a mate with many of the same characteristics. She knew this relationship was bad for her in many ways but could not free herself from it. In describing why she stayed, she said, "I don't have to bury my mother."

While most of us have some vague notion of chemistry and what it entails, we ask the question, at one time or another,

"Why am I so attracted to him or her? I seem to keep getting involved with the same type of person, even though they are bad for me."

As we all know, history repeats itself in more ways than one. In terms of a relationship, we all repeat our past. By past, I mean our relationships with the significant others in our lives, usually our parents.

We repeat our past in an attempt to master it. The notion is that we will try again and again until it comes out right. One of the earliest childhood defenses is to blame ourselves. We do this because it is safer to believe that there is something wrong with us, not our parents. From the point of view of a child, this makes total sense. Parents are our whole world and it is very scary to think that there is something wrong with them because it would mean that our entire world is unsafe. Also, if there is something wrong with our parents, who are our entire world, we are helpless to fix it. But, if there is something wrong with us, we can fix it. Thus comes the battle cry of so many relationships; "What did I do wrong? If only they let me know, then I could do something about it." This is an unconscious process and occurs automatically, as do so many of our reactions later on. Blaming oneself and trying to fix what's wrong all go back to an early period in life when we truly believed this could be done.

It is important to remember that, at one time, this way of thinking and behaving was adaptive. It helped us to survive in a difficult or unlivable situation. However, these adaptive ways become maladaptive later on as we try to change our mates and change ourselves to please them.

CHAPTER II

FATAL ATTRACTIONS

As I noted earlier, we are attracted to others based on our personal history. When it is problematic, as many are, our relationships will be such. I refer to these as fatal attractions. Fatal because they are destructive or, at best, problematic and it is hard to extricate oneself. You may ask, if it is so difficult, why not end it? The answer is that problematic relationships have a way of taking over and hooking you in. Because they often undermine you, it is even harder to leave.

While there are as many fatal attractions as there are people, there seem to be some basic themes that permeate them. These include attraction to the unavailable, the hopeless dreamer, the person who promises everything and gives nothing, etc. I will present a few such types that I feel embody many of the characteristics of these fatal attractions.

---

1. The lure of the unavailable: Hooked on hope

Many ask, "Why am I attracted to someone who rejects me?" Let me elaborate by saying that rejection can take many forms. A partner might be unloving, unreliable or emotionally unavailable in some other way. They might be physically present but not truly there, not listening or responding to their partner. They might always shift the focus onto their own self, leaving their partner to feel abandoned.

The end result is the same. You are left hungry and wanting. It is like having your dinner plate snatched away before you can finish. The rest of the night you are hungry. You might dream about food or the gourmet meal you would love to have.

Any need left unfulfilled grows in intensity. A relationship that is depriving can leave you feeling half starved. As a result, you crave that person even more. It underlies the attraction many have to a married person.

Lara was a tall, slender woman with a wild sort of beauty. She would look up at the sky with joy. Her thick honey colored hair would fly in the breeze like a lion's mane. She was in love with nature. She was in love with life. She was also in love with a married man who adored her as well. But he was unavailable most of the time. When she first met him, she had just freed herself from an abusive marriage. She was beginning to feel strong and, true to her nature, she began to embrace life with a passion that drew others to her. And so, she drew John to her.

They both were vacationing at a seaside town, Lara with her children and John with his wife. She was standing by the dunes, breathing in the salt air and luxuriating in the sunshine she so loved when John spotted her. Their eyes met and both felt an intensity they had never known. Phone numbers were exchanged. Lara told herself this would be nothing but a casual relationship and half believed this self-deception. Little by little, she was sucked into a nightmare of longings that could never be fulfilled. Their clandestine meetings always ended abruptly as he raced home to his suspicious wife. Lara lived for these brief encounters and dreaded their abrupt endings.

The highlight of their relationship took place one warm summer afternoon. For three hours, they went fishing in a small boat.

"We didn't even have to talk … we just looked at each other and knew each other's thoughts … we were like one," she said. Lara would reminisce over this fishing trip for years.

Meetings remained brief. He would cancel at the last minute, not return phone calls, and made promises he could not keep. They began to argue violently. Then it would end. "It was like I was the sole survivor of an earthquake," she said to me when describing how she felt as each ending would occur. She would call him frantically but he would not answer. When he did, an argument would ensue. She would then become determined to end their relationship. Then her cell phone would ring repeatedly, sometimes dozens of times in a row. Her life consisted of brief meetings and clutching her cell phone, desperately awaiting his call. This went on for years. She fell into a deep depression and became almost unable to function.

One day I listened as a friend asked, "What is so great about this man?" Lara relayed her memory of the fishing trip and what joy she felt. Her voice was dreamlike as she recounted this memory. It was as though she were in a trance. "So your life has been whittled down to three hours?" was her friend's reply. Lara seemed not to hear this. She was lost in reverie. She longed for him, longed for that exquisite happiness she felt when she was connected to him.

This sort of longing that Lara felt had grown into a passionate desire for him. He had become idealized, romanticized and larger than life. "He is the most beautiful thing that God ever created," she once said. She was not seeing him for who he truly was. Instead, he was the embodiment of all her needs and desires.

What would have helped Lara would have been to see that this was more about her own passions and desires than about who he truly was. For, during moments of sound reflection, she admitted that he could be selfish, inconsiderate and egotistical.

We often mistake longing for love. Longing comes from unmet needs. Love, on the other hand, is the presence of true caring affection. As a result, it might not seem as exciting or enticing. What is more enticing than something that is just out of reach?

Lara admitted that he frequently behaved in an unloving way. When she was sick or stranded in a broken down car, he was usually not available. He would be off in a bar or socializing with friends while she frantically reached out for his help. Need after need remained unmet until she felt half starved.

There is another piece at work. It is the notion of intermittent reinforcement. That simply means that one receives a reward on an intermittent basis. Being intermittent, it is random and inconsistent. It is the psychology behind gambling. Every so often, the gambler randomly receives a reward for their constant funneling of money into a slot machine or through some other means. They keep trying because they know that, at some point in time, that monetary reward will come; they just don't know when. So they keep trying and trying, hoping for that big payoff.

Lara was enslaved by this sort of random, intermittent reinforcement. She never knew when he would be available. So she would keep trying, hoping for that magic moment when he would appear on her doorstep, ready to lavish her with passion.

Perpetuating this type of interaction enables one to keep hope alive, hope that one day you will receive your reward.

Lara dreamed of the day when John would leave his wife and they would be together for good. She fantasized about the beautiful house they would have together, the magical holidays and vacations they would have, the delicious meals they would share every night and what it would be like to wake up with him by her side every morning. She hung onto this hope for dear life. She was hooked.

The one who is unavailable

Why would someone be perpetually unavailable? Why give just enough to keep your partner hooked on hope? It is important to realize that the unavailable one doesn't necessarily mean to be rejecting. They are probably afraid of intimacy and fearful of commitment. Why? Usually the answer is that their sense of self is precarious, which makes them afraid of fully entering into a relationship for fear of losing themself. We often describe such a person as *"commitment phobic."*

Although there may be many reasons for commitment phobia it usually comes down to one basic idea. That person is afraid of losing themself in a relationship. Realistically, we do give up some of our independence in a relationship. Your sense of self must be strong enough to deal with this. If it is not, you will feel easily controlled and taken over. In essence, you feel like you are losing yourself. You become frightened and often resentful. You might lash out at your partner for no good reason. Your partner will feel bewildered and confused, often wondering, "What did I do to upset him or her?" The answer usually is "nothing." This is hard to get.

Also, you yourself might harbor the same fears; fears of losing yourself, of being crowded or invaded. By staying with a depriving person, you do not have to confront your own fears of intimacy.

The deadly dance

Often, two people will engage in a dance of chase and flee. The unavailable one stirs up anxiety in their partner with their disappearing acts. This causes their partner to pursue them even more which causes the other to move even farther away. If the pursuer backs off, the unavailable one may then begin to do the chasing.

Nancy was a lively, outspoken woman who was married to a man who was perpetually unavailable, physically and emotionally. He would go bowling three times a week without her and spend the rest of his spare time fixing up other people's houses while neglecting his own. Most people loved him. He was forever available to remodel someone's bathroom or fix a stubborn leak. He was there for everyone except his wife. He'd fix any problem in anyone's home except his own. When he was with his wife, he was emotionally unavailable and would respond to her attempts to engage him by retreating into himself and giving her vague, one word answers. All of this naturally enraged his wife, which caused her to nag and become confrontational. She had started following him to the bowling alley even though she didn't bowl. She would simply sit there while he interacted with everyone but her. The more she pursued and confronted, the more he fled. He never asked where she would go or show any interest in her. He took for granted that she would be there. I advised her to back off. No more trips to the bowling alley. In fact, she packed her bags one weekend and, without explanation, went to her sister's house. When she came home, she did not engage him at all. She went about her business and said nothing.

Slowly but surely, he began to pursue her. He started to question where she went and sought out her company more and more.

This is a very typical pattern that many couples engage in, and greatly illustrates the way in which you can get hooked on the unavailable.

You do not really know your own limits until you are with someone who is truly there. Sometimes the person who is truly there does not seem as appealing or exciting. There is not that intensity of excitement that arises when your needs are only partially met. As I said, when your dinner plate is always snatched away before you are done, you do not get to know your satiation level. But a good, tasty meal that is not taken away until you are satisfied does not leave you with the same sense of longing that feeds this excitement. If you waited until satisfied, you would not continue to keep eating.

2. The hopeless dreamer: Hooked on fantasy

We paint with the brush of illusion
The one whom we think we love

~Anonymous

The world of the internet certainly attests to the basic truth
that many people are hooked on fantasy.

So often, out in the singles scene, you will see people endlessly
pursuing someone. Once they have them, they don't want
them. They either become disinterested or frightened when
the other person moves too close for comfort. We call them
many things: hopeless dreamers, incurable romantics, etc.
They all boil down to the same concept. You are with
someone who is more involved in their own head than they
are with you.

What is responsible for this phenomenon? We have total
control over our fantasies and the persons in them. But real
life doesn't work that way. We have minimal control over
many things, especially other people. In your head, the other
person can be exactly as you want them to be. They can fulfill
all your needs, be totally attuned to you and you never have
to worry about being rejected. When you have had enough
contact, you can simply turn off the fantasy switch.

Peter always wanted just enough contact to keep his vivid
fantasies alive. Too much contact would ultimately kill these
wild fantasies. We would spend a romantic evening together, but
there would always be some point at which he couldn't wait to

get home. I wouldn't hear from him for days. He later revealed that, when he would get home, he would fantasize about me all night. In fact, he fantasized about me morning and night. When I tried to get closer to him and said that this arrangement wasn't satisfactory for me, he seemed genuinely mystified. "But I think about you all the time ... all my fantasies are about you." "Yes," I'd say, "but the only problem is that I don't live in your head so it isn't doing me a hell of a lot of good."

---

3. Falling for false promises

Marissa was a vivacious redhead who laughed easily and had a heart of gold. She was in love with a man who needled her and dangled the proverbial carrot in front of her nose. He would be loving one day and rejecting the next. His cruel remarks constantly undermined her sense of self. He compared her to other women, with her falling short, and abandoned her on many occasions. They broke up twice. After the first breakup, she was very depressed and questioned herself continuously. Yet there was that chemistry.

He wheedled his way back into her life and they went on a vacation together, a vacation that she had originally planned for herself. He seduced her with fantasies of the wonderful time they would share. Once they arrived at the resort, his true colors surfaced once again. While there were some magical moments, they deteriorated as the vacation progressed. When they arrived home, the relationship rapidly unraveled for the last time.

Marissa continually asked herself questions. "Maybe if I worked harder this wouldn't have happened," she would say to herself.

In such scenarios, there is the desire to undo, remake, go over, and "fix" whatever went wrong. But none of these efforts work since the heart does not listen to logic or reason. It listens to feelings, passions and desires, whether or not they make sense.

When the final blow came, Marissa was as shocked as she was the first time around even though it was clear that it was inevitable. Intellectually, she knew he was bad for her and that she needed to move on. Despite the fact that he was deficient in so many areas and incapable of an intimate relationship, a fact she knew, she continued to go over the vacation in her mind, asking, "But why did he do that ... everything was fine ... nothing was wrong." What she really meant was that she did nothing wrong; she was trying to convince herself of this fact and having a very difficult time believing it.

If another woman were to come to Marissa for advice, presenting the same scenario, she would tell her to leave that man. But when you are caught up in it yourself, it is so difficult to be objective.

We all have dreams and fantasies about our ideal mate and ideal life. We envision our ideal mate based on our history and needs. We may picture someone handsome, beautiful, strong, sensitive, nurturing, take charge, sophisticated, witty, down-to-earth, someone who shares our interests and sensibilities. The list of adjectives is as large as human imagination. We so want to believe that this wonderful person can come along that we often blind ourselves to reality.

Intellectually, Marissa knew the truth about this man. But she could not let herself feel the reality of the situation. To do so would be to let go of a dream. And so she fell for one empty promise after another in order to keep this dream alive.

Hope enlivens us and keeps us striving for our dreams. Loss of hope can lead to depression and even death in the case of a serious illness. At any rate, it is a terrible state and we will do anything to avoid it. Thus, when someone comes along who promises to fulfill our dreams, emotions take over and keep us from seeing the truth.

Most people would admit that they are not totally themselves upon meeting someone they like. We want to make a good impression, to put on our best show. As someone once said, "How much longer can I be this enchanting creature?" referring to her attempts to impress a man whom she hoped to win over.

———————

4. The knight in shining armor

"I promise you the moon."

"It is lovely that you'll promise me the moon, but the moon isn't what I'm asking for."

The knight in shining armor, in some ways, is a spinoff of the person who fills you with false promises, but with a special twist. Mr. Perfect comes galloping towards you, dazzling you with promises of wondrous things. He seems to intuitively know your every need, dream and desire and assures you that he is just the ticket.

I met Irwin at a dance. He seemed sensitive, funny and solici-
tous. He was very engaging and seemed genuinely enchanted
by me. He drove me home. As we approached the steps to my
house, he saw one of my cats disappear under a bush. He
knew I was worried about the cat and had been looking for
him. He disregarded his fine clothes and darted under the
bush after the cat, saying, "I love cats." I was very taken in by
this gesture.

The next week we went out to dinner. As we entered the
restaurant, he put my hand gently on the counter near the
coat check-in, intuiting my need to be grounded and not left
standing in the void of my blindness. Unlike the man I had
been dating up to that point, who was always only too happy
to hand me half the bill, he was generous. I had a couple of
glasses of fine wine and he was sure to ask me if I wanted
appetizers, side dishes, dessert, etc. We then went dancing.
Everything seemed magical.

A week after we met, a blizzard was headed our way. Irwin
called to ask what I needed to stock up on for the storm. He
galloped to my doorstep laden with delicious meals, tasty
treats and flowers. After the storm arrived, he was only too
eager to shovel my walkway.

When I came down with the flu, I had an endless supply of
chicken soup, fruit juices, and comfort food as well as
medication. He always reminded me that he was only ten
minutes away and to please call him any time of day or night
if I needed him.

Valentine's Day I was graced with not one, but three dozen
roses, and Irwin dressed up as a florist.

I was wined, dined, and taken care of.

However, phone calls started to come a little too often, sometimes three times in rapid succession. I tried to slow down the pace, which was not easy. As we got more involved, he tried to shower me with all kinds of things. He wanted to buy me a new coat, insisting that my full-length leather coat was not flattering. I told him I was happy with my coat and didn't need a new one. He was dying to take me on a cruise. I told him a cruise wasn't very good for me since I'd have to leave my guide dog behind and there was too much shuffling around with a cruise, getting on and off the ship. I would always tell him what I wanted but he seemed not to hear.

He always had some notion of what I should want; a cruise, expensive clothes, etc. I wanted some simple things for the house to make my life easier and a simple vacation in a plain cottage by the shore. In fact, just take me to the local beach.

Beware of people who come at you too fast and too soon. They often are not seeing you for who you truly are. Instead, they are taken in by some characteristic of yours which they embellish with their own fantasies which are fueled by a bottomless pit of unmet needs. You become idealized and eventually uncomfortable when you see that the person is not seeing you for who you truly are, but, rather, who they would like you to be.

So often, we try to force-fit the other person to fit our fantasies and dreams, which inevitably leads to resentment. This happened with Irwin.

He could not see that what I needed most of all was companionship and emotional connection. Let's share a bottle of wine by the fire and talk. He would sit for five minutes and then jump up, saying he had to go to the store to get something he just knew I would love.

We got into endless squabbles about everything. Whatever I wanted or did, he seemed to have something fancier or better. I did not feel listened to or understood. I was lonely. I told him that he was trying to turn me into some ideal image he had in his head.

My needs started to irritate him and his attempts to turn me into the princess he dreamed of grated on my nerves.

The princess turned into an ordinary woman and the knight fell off his horse.

CHAPTER III
RED FLAGS AND
WHAT WE DO WITH THEM

It is not just what we are attracted to, but what we choose to ignore that perpetuates these problematic relationships. What we choose to ignore are the red flags that signal what is to come. In reviewing many of my relationships and those of clients and friends, I realize that red flags were there from the very beginning. Some surfaced in the first meeting and virtually all surfaced in the first few weeks. We rationalize them away; the truth is we don't really know what they mean. Sometimes the things that you think will be an issue are not but something else is.

Why do we ignore these red flags? We don't consciously ignore them. Instead, it is a more automatic process in which we misinterpret, fail to see or otherwise rationalize them away. There are a number of reasons for this. First, you might fail to see a red flag because you are so used to a certain behavior. For example, you may have grown up with parents who perpetually gave you double messages or were critical, invalidating or unresponsive. As a result, these traits will seem normal and natural to you.

I can't tell you how many clients have asked me, "But doesn't every relationship have a lot of conflict or fighting? Isn't it normal that he didn't call me back when he said he would… don't all men do this?"

Another reason is the desire to hold onto hope. Most will agree that it is hard to find someone with whom you "click," where there is that chemistry or connection. It is hard to give up on your hopes and dreams. We want for it to work so much that we blind ourselves to the realities, right from the very beginning.

What are some of the red flags that tip me off to the fact that something is wrong with my relationship?

1. Excessive Anxiety

Freud was one of the first to identify anxiety as a signal that something is wrong. It is a warning sign that there is some feeling we are not addressing. It may be the feeling that your mate is not really for you. It may be the fear of losing your mate that can arise from different sources. For example, you may be afraid that asserting yourself or addressing something that is bothering you will cause your mate to reject you. At any rate, it is telling you that something isn't right and you need to pay closer attention.

2. Irritability

Another red flag is irritability. Often, when I see couples, one or both will complain that some specific behavior irritates them. It can be as little as their mate leaving empty bottles or crumbs on the counter. The one doing the complaining will often be upset with themselves for being distressed over something they see as trivial. I then say it is not the event but what it signifies. The event or action may be small but what it represents is not. What I often hear is, "He knows it bothers me, so why does he keep doing it?" The underlying issue may be that the mate feels dismissed or is upset by the lack of consideration. Or, they may feel that their feelings are not respected in general.

3. Overanalyzing

When you find yourself dissecting your relationship, it is a sure sign that something is wrong. This behavior arises from anxiety. It often represents an attempt to understand and gain control of things over which you have no control. It is good to understand and reflect but when it goes too far and turns into a habit of analyzing your mate's behaviors under a microscope, it is a sign that something is fundamentally wrong. Unfortunately, this often turns into unproductive wheel spinning. I often say, "You are on a hamster wheel," and this usually resonates with the person doing the wheel spinning.

The goal is to get off the hamster wheel and to sit quietly and pay attention to your gut reactions. They speak the truth and rarely lead you down the wrong path.

4. Feeling jerked around

When you feel like you are being jerked around, you probably are. It is a sure sign that there is some ambivalence on the part of your mate.

When I was dating Peter, he would always end the night and make a date for another saying, "I'll pencil you in." This bothered me, but I all too quickly dismissed this remark. He would only make dates for Tuesday and Saturday nights. I remember someone asking me why I never see Peter on Friday night. I didn't have an answer. Others told me they saw him at singles' socials on Friday nights. When I asked Peter about this, he said he just liked to see his friends. In retrospect, I was amazed at how I ignored all of this even though it nagged at me. I always felt shoehorned in but quickly dismissed this feeling in order to preserve this dysfunctional relationship.

5. Ambivalence

Ambivalence that surfaces early on in a relationship rarely, if ever subsides. It is a sign that something is wrong, that you or your mate are not comfortable with something in the relationship. Unfortunately, by the time it surfaces, you are already hooked and don't want to admit that there is a problem.

Of course these are just a few examples of red flags. The main idea is that something isn't sitting right with you and you should pay attention to your gut reactions. This is not always easy since it can be hard to sort out what comes from your own issues and what comes from the relationship. Intimate relationships bring out one's issues, making the sorting out tricky. Becoming aware of your triggers helps with this whole process.

When I described my relationship with Jim early in this book, I said I saw subtle signs that something was wrong but, in retrospect, they seemed obvious. This included him saying, "You think so," in an ominous tone when I threw my arms around him and said he was a sweetie. I knew I felt something was off, but I did not pay attention. I am now convinced that the dream that followed, the one where I tried to call him but the phone frizzled into so many scorched pieces, was a red flag.

PART THREE

The Healing Heart

Although the title of this book is, *Getting Over a Broken Heart*, I must elaborate by saying that the notion of "getting over" is somewhat of a misconception. People often say "get over it," "move on," or "snap out of it." These are words no one wants to hear since they invalidate your feelings and don't really speak the truth. The truth is that you don't "just get over it." I often remind clients that "it" is not a cold; you don't simply catch it and then get over it. By "it," I mean the pain of the loss. Someone once said that each loss leaves a little hole. You move on but it is a part of you forever. You live with it, work around it but you don't "get over it."

The notion of getting over something is so much a Western one with its focus on curing things, eradicating them forever in some aggressive manner. A better notion is that of healing. How do we heal?

Healing is a slow process that unfolds over time. As much as you might like, you cannot fast forward to a future time.

Realizing this and allowing yourself to experience all of your feelings is essential. You need to allow yourself the chance to grieve. What does this mean? It means to allow yourself the full range of feelings connected with the loss which will include shock, sadness, anger, etc. Everyone grieves differently and there is not a set formula or set sequence of stages. As I explained in Part One, grief is different from depression. Depression and anxiety, although normal when experiencing a loss, are not truly feelings, they are states that reflect distortions of feelings.

Although depression can sometimes serve a protective function by numbing you to the pain, it ultimately pulls you away from yourself and is thus a poor solution.

CHAPTER I
RECLAIM YOURSELF

I live again remembering nicer days
Before I lost myself along the way

~Anonymous

1. In love with being alone

We lose a part of ourself in a relationship. This is the price of intimacy.

When I broke up with Ed, a man with whom I was involved for a brief time, I experienced a certain liberation after the initial trauma. This relationship was on the heels of a more devastating breakup, which fueled the pain and blow to my inner self. Somehow, I knew Ed wasn't truly the man for me. I often found myself getting irritated with him, wishing he would shut up when he would ramble on about nothing for hours. Yet there was passion, at least in the very beginning and a certain comfort. We shared some wonderful days and nights together, dining, cuddling, taking long walks and talks about all sorts of things. We had become a part of each other.

Thus, when it ended suddenly we both felt devastated, like we had lost a piece of ourselves.

After a couple of months, I decided to go to a convention in Los Angeles, just myself and my guide dog Hope. While I was anxious, there was a lot of excitement. After an arduous journey, I was settled comfortably in my hotel. I sat out on the patio and ordered lunch. I'll never forget the exhilaration, the sense of total freedom and well being that I had. I was in love with being alone. In fact, I was a little disgruntled when others would invite me to have dinner with them, knowing they probably felt bad for the blind woman sitting alone. I'm sure they never in a million years dreamed that I was happy to be alone. I had reclaimed myself and did not want to give it up for anyone, not even to have lunch or dinner.

2. Feel your own self-worth

Earlier, I described my relationship with Jim and the marked difference between the depression I felt when he rejected me versus the grief I felt when he died. What enabled me to begin to get over the depression that resulted from the initial breakup?

First, let's look at the breakup, how it happened and what it did to me. He called me up and said that he cared about me but was not in love with me, that he wanted to get married and have kids and couldn't see doing this with someone who was going blind. In retrospect, I can see that part of the devastation was the blow to my self-esteem. First, I was told that he was not in love with me which is a blow in and of itself. It drummed up any feelings of unlovability and inadequacy that I might have been harboring. In addition, I was just informed that I would not make an adequate parent because of my eyesight. Another blow to the self. He had said, "How will you take care of a child?" I now believe that he was wondering how I would take care of him. In other words, instead of internalizing his remarks and blaming myself, I shifted the focus to where it belonged; on to him. Indeed, he was, in many ways, inadequate. He could not take care of himself, let alone a child.

Three weeks after the breakup, he called me up, asking me to come over for his birthday. I knew he just wanted sex. I let him know that he had some nerve calling me up after what he just did. I also said, "There are many totally blind couples who raise kids." I was indignant. My sense of self reared up, shouting its worth. It was then that I felt better.

Feelings of worthlessness, unlovability and inadequacy are so much a part of depression. When I was able to get in touch with my own feelings of self-worth and express them I was able to move on.

CHAPTER II
EMBRACE YOUR FEAR
AND PAIN

Depression is also about loss of connection, connection to your loved one and connection to your own self. That is why it is so important to stay in touch with all of your feelings, no matter how painful or frightening and to have compassion for your wounded self.

My breakup with Alex greatly illustrates this latter point. I remember the first glimmer of hope I felt amidst the exquisite pain. As I said I experienced not just the loss of him but the loss of all the dreams and hopes that the relationship embodied. The glimmer came when I was sitting in a chair and allowing myself to feel all my feelings. I felt the incredible hurt and the pain of my loss of self. Then a strange thing happened; I fell in love with myself. I was completely in touch with my fragility, vulnerability, hurt and felt total compassion for the wounded person who was me.

Often, after a breakup, a person will berate themselves. As I said earlier, you may blame yourself, second guess yourself and work and re-work the breakup. What did I do wrong…, did I make the right decision…, why doesn't he or she love me anymore, and so on and so forth.

Anxiety, on the other hand, arises from many sources. It can arise out of fear of loss of a relationship, fear of a loss of one's self and fear that you will be stuck in the same pattern and never be able to move on to something better.

The breakup of a relationship is such a disorganizing experience. It throws you into chaos, turmoil and disrupts your sense of self, which is very frightening. You are not just losing that person, but the part of you that is enmeshed in that relationship.

Many people experience anxiety attacks after the loss of a relationship. Numerous buttons get pushed, such as fear of abandonment and the fear of no one being there for you in a time of need.

There is a whole period of disorganization of one's self that comes about with any loss of a relationship. You may feel tempted to fill up the void with anything.You may be tempted to dive right into another relationship. But the best thing you can do is to just sit with yourself, to allow yourself to experience the fear and pain, even though this is very difficult. How does one do this difficult task?

Having compassion for yourself and embracing your pain and fear is the beginning. In our society, we tend to run away from pain. We seem to have the notion that we are supposed to be happy all the time and that any form of suffering is a terrible waste of your life. This reminds me of a great sermon I heard on the radio. I don't remember the name of the minister but he said something to the effect that, since the pursuit of happiness inevitably makes us miserable, we may as well try to be miserable. He then outlined numerous steps to misery. Hilarious but so true. We all know the basic truth that we shouldn't try to be something we are not. However, we often fail to take the next step which is, don't try to feel something you don't really feel. If you are sad, be sad. Grief and sadness are an important part of life.

There is also another aspect of grief. Allowing yourself to fully grieve and go over the trauma again and again eventually lessens the impact.

"At what point do I stop?" people often ask. "I find myself wallowing in misery...I think about it night and day...my mind goes around in circles and my thoughts scare me."

This isn't grief as much as it is an obsessive thought pattern. Obsessive thoughts actually pull you away from yourself and your feelings. Sitting quietly and stilling your mind allows your feelings to surface. The nature of any feeling is that it comes and goes in waves, it is never a constant. This is something to keep in mind. The intense pain, when you allow it to run its course, will not stay with you all the time.

Talking about it can release your feelings or pull you away from them. Listen to your inner voice. It will tell you when talking is counterproductive.

I remember how, with Alex, I talked and talked. I would initially feel a sense of relief but it was always short-lived. As soon as I was quiet, the pain would surface full force. Then I would reach for the phone until I ran out of people to call. Instead of reaching for the phone, I needed to reach inside. It was the one day when, instead of reaching for the phone for the twentieth time, I reached inside that I got in touch with the part of me that loves myself and was able to embrace my pain. This truly strengthened me and gave me relief.

CHAPTER III

HEALING EXERCISES

1. Still your mind

This is especially a challenge for a person with a busy mind which is true of most of us. However, it is helpful to work towards this goal. How?

You can sit in a quiet place, close your eyes and focus on the sensation of air leaving your nostrils. To anchor your thoughts, you can count each exhalation until you get to ten. Then start over again. When your mind wanders, gently bring it back to your breathing.

Or, you can visualize a particular scene or object. It can be as simple as a green square. You simply focus your mind on it and bring your attention back to it when it wanders.

I remember a particular session with a client who was severely depressed after a breakup. What she didn't know was that I was also going through a similar situation. I taught her these techniques and together we meditated. Then something magical happened. We looked at each other and smiled and laughed and silently shared a feeling of peace and joy as the black cloud of depression lifted.

If you think of what is involved in the learning process, these exercises make great sense. When you are trying to memorize something, you go over it and over it until it leaves a little crease in your brain. The constant repetition of a thought only serves to strengthen it.

2. Examine your relationship

This applies to the breakup of a dysfunctional relationship. Look at it with a critical eye. Just the fact that it ended tells you there was something wrong with it. So often people say everything was fine, but obviously this is not true or it wouldn't have ended.

3. Intellect versus feeling

Processing the loss of a relationship is so hard to do. In the case of a breakup, you may intellectually dissect it and come up with a long list of flaws in your former mate that are designed to make you feel that "it is all for the best." You may get angry, disgusted and, for a moment, feel relieved that it ended. It's funny how people often say, "It wasn't meant to be" in their attempts to soothe themselves or a friend. Yet, I have found that, from my own personal experience, this tends to fall on deaf ears. I have tried to analyze why this is so. My belief is that it doesn't work because it comes from an intellectual place as opposed to an emotional one. The thought is "Yes, I know this person is bad for me" while the feeling is "I still love and miss them and want them back." One cannot reconcile such a dichotomy. It is best to realize that it is okay to feel this way and you need to allow yourself to feel the way you do.

The case of Marissa, described earlier, illustrates this well. As I stated, she intellectually knew he was bad for her, that the breakup was inevitable and that she needed to move on. Yet she continued to ask, "but why did he do that...everything was fine...nothing was wrong."

She could not integrate her intellect and emotions. As I have elaborated, the heart doesn't listen to reason, it listens to feelings, passions and desires, whether or not they make sense. She could easily advise another woman to leave such a toxic relationship but could not follow her own advice since emotions are more powerful.

Many say, "Listen to your gut." I think of the gut as your inner voice. It is your true self which is in touch with all your thoughts and feelings and usually does not lead you in the wrong direction.

4. Don't beat yourself up

An added component that keeps you stuck in your misery and painful ruminations in the case of a breakup may be that you still blame yourself for the breakup and think that there is something that you could have done to fix things. As I noted earlier, this comes from your childhood belief that, if your parents reject or hurt you emotionally, it must be your fault. Being your fault, you then feel you can fix it. When you realize this is the source and can begin to let go of that childhood fantasy, you are halfway there. It is a two way street and you cannot control your partner's actions.

5. Write down your thoughts and feelings

Writing releases feelings and puts you in touch with your inner self while at the same time giving you a certain objectivity. Many, including myself, find this to be a very liberating process. It is why some people keep journals that allow them to express all their thoughts and feelings without worrying about negative feedback from others or some other type of consequence.

6. Get angry

Ge angry. You have been hurt and are entitled to be angry. You don't have to justify it and the anger doesn't have to be rational. It doesn't matter if the loss is through death or a breakup. It is just as natural to be angry at a loved one who dies since they left you. This is a time to throw your intellect away and allow yourself, as I have said earlier, to feel all of your feelings without worrying whether or not they make sense.

There is another aspect of anger that is healing. Anger cannot exist side by side with depression or anxiety. I often tell clients who suffer from anxiety attacks to think of something that makes them angry. The anxiety inevitably goes away. The same applies for depression.

Anger can be very strengthening. It is enlivening and reflects a wounded self that is shouting its outrage and reclaiming its rights.

Janet experienced a blow that would have flattened many. After having a baby with what seemed to be her doting fiancé,

he informed her that he no longer loved her, that he loved
someone else and was going to leave. What was even worse
was that he was rejecting the baby. She was in a state of shock
for a week or so. After the reality of it all registered, this shock
gave way to hurt and outrage. She let him know, in no uncer-
tain terms, that he had hurt her deeply. There was righteous
indignation in her voice as she relayed the exchange to me.
There was no pretense; she was hurt and he was going to
know how much. She was authentic, true to her feelings and
not at all ashamed of them. This gave her the strength needed
to move on.

7. Take action

There is nothing worse than being in a passive, waiting mode.
I addressed this when describing my conflict over whether or
not to call Alex, who had rejected me and did not call as he
said he would. As I said, if I had it to do over, I would have
called him after a few days of processing things and I would
have been true to my feelings. Janet, whom I just described,
was totally authentic, true to her feelings and not afraid to
express them. This helped her to heal.

8. Feed yourself

What makes you happy? After a relationship has ended and
you are in the depths of sorrow your answer will probably be
"nothing." However, as my own mother would remind me, I
had lived, survived and thrived a number of years before I
even knew him. It is strange that it never feels that way. You
lose all perspective and the present seems as though it has

been here forever. That is the nature of depression. The fact is that it is a temporary state and is not the truth. There was a time when you were happy. Just the fact that you were able to experience such happiness at the beginning of the relationship shows you that you have the capacity for such happiness. Also, there are things that make you happy. Do them. Even if they don't make you happy at this time, do them anyway and you will slowly but surely start to reclaim parts of yourself.

This is also about loving yourself, being gentle with yourself and embracing all parts of yourself, especially your wounded self.

9. Restore structure

Restore a sense of normalcy. As I said earlier, the loss of a loved one is such a disorganizing experience that it completely throws you off track.

10. Reframe negative thoughts

We sometimes label certain thoughts, feelings or traits as bad. However, when viewed in a different light, they can be seen as positive. For example, a person may call his or herself needy. Rather than saying I am needy, try saying I need a lot and want a lot, I am a passionate, sensitive person and want to have a full, rich life.

11. Role play

Pretend you are another person giving you comfort and advice. I have done this and so have many of my clients and friends. This helps bring you in touch with the part of you that loves you. It also gives that much needed objectivity, the ability to step outside yourself and gain perspective.

CHAPTER IV

CASE HISTORIES

In the remainder of this book I will present two people who exemplify many of the points I have outlined so far.

1. Justin

Justin was a highly intelligent, sensitive and successful man who fell into a state of depression and severe anxiety after the sudden breakup of a relationship. He had early morning awakenings with obsessive thoughts and a fear of the future. He would wake up at 4 in the morning and ruminate over the breakup.

I asked if he liked to write and said that it releases one's feelings while giving distance at the same time. He knew what I meant. He shared that he used to journal and write poetry.

I suggested that, when he wakes up at 4 a.m., and starts to ruminate, he should get up , make his coffee and start writing. I said he should be gentle with himself and that one of the things that feeds the pain is the blow to oneself. This really resonated with him. I shared how someone once said to me that it seemed like the only person who could make it better is the one who caused it in the first place. He totally related to this notion.

The next time we met, he said he had started waking up, making his coffee and writing and this helped him a great deal. However, he then said he felt pressured to get out there and socialize. He had looked up the words shy and introverted and realized he was introverted. I sensed he was down on himself for this. I then told him about a great book in which the author said that to be shy is to be tender. He came alive when I said this.

This is an example of reframing. We took what he perceived as a negative trait and reframed it as something very positive.

We shared our mutual fear of public speaking and how we both avoided classes in which you had to get up and talk. "I'd rather take a twelve hour test," I said. He laughed and said he felt the same.

I asked if he had ever seen the movie *The 40-Year-Old Virgin*, and he said he only saw part of it. I said how guys around the main character pressured him to be something he wasn't, and in the end, a girl loved him for who he was.

These are all examples of embracing all parts of yourself and loving yourself as well as reframing. He learned to accept and love all parts of himself without judgment.

When we went over his relationship history, it became clear that he had been involved with some aggressive women.

Instead of beating himself up for just being his own shy self and blaming himself for the failed relationships, he looked at the other person. Before, he overvalued the woman who broke his heart and was unable to see any flaws in her although he had no trouble finding flaws or perceived flaws in himself. This new found ability to shift the focus onto the other person strengthened his sense of self.

He started to go on dating sites and was dismayed at the ways in which some of the women would go on and on about their travels, and life. He said so many of the ads say, "Looking for someone positive, upbeat, etc." I said that maybe he should put an ad in saying, "Downer, negative, cup is half empty, introvert, hate travel." We both laughed.

He became distressed about well-meaning friends who would tell him, "She was no good for you," and they would give a million examples of why this was so. This never works because, as I have said, it comes from an intellectual place and the heart doesn't listen to reason, it listens to feelings, passions and desires, whether or not they make sense.

In subsequent sessions he expressed his dismay that he still missed his ex, knowing all the problems inherent in their relationship. I said, "That is because when you lose someone, you don't just lose all the bad things, you lose the good things as well."

He then went over the good things he missed such as affection and nurturance. This helped him to understand why he still missed her. He admitted she did meet some needs and he missed that part. I said our goal is for him to meet someone who can meet these needs without having all of the very negative traits. I suggested putting in an internet ad that says, "fuzzy, not crazy," since many of these ads are anything but warm and fuzzy.

Also, this points to the fact that one cannot be talked out of one's feelings. He realized it was okay to miss her and feel sad and lonely at times. This is all part of accepting your whole self.

He really started to question his attachment and what it was that hooked him. I asked if it was the person or the functions and needs she fulfilled to which he was attached. This helped clarify his attachment. As I have stated, love is not attachment and seeing this helped.

He later spoke of how he gets attached to women who choose him, not women he chooses. He realized that after he received a compliment from a woman and he was taken in by her. This was a red flag to which he needed to pay attention and reflected a lot of self-awareness.

Justin's experiences embody so many of the points that have been described. First, there was the intensity of the pain. He would describe the shock of waking up at 4 a.m. and having the pain hit him full force. He spoke of how his thoughts would race. As I have said, it is natural to go over and over the breakup but when it becomes obsessive as it did with Justin, the goal is to pull oneself out of the obsessive thought train. That was when the journaling and redirecting of his thoughts helped.

When I addressed the blow to his self-esteem, a lightbulb went off in his head and he truly started to understand that such a blow fueled his terrible pain. I saw how he was down on himself for being shy and self conscious. I saw how he pressured himself to be something he was not. In a sense, I let him know it is okay to be shy or self-conscious around groups of people. Ironically, giving himself permission to just be who he is helped him to become more open because the pressure was off and he did not have to please anyone or pretend to be something he was not. One important thing I should mention is the role of humor. The fact that we were both able to find humor in some of this helped to normalize his feelings.

When he started to embrace his pain and become more gentle with himself, he began to truly feel better. One of the problems was that so many of his friends tried to convince him that his ex was no good and he shouldn't be upset since it was good that they broke up. As I have said, you cannot talk anyone out of their feelings. The notion that she was no good for him didn't help since it came from an intellectual place, not an emotional place. It is not until we dive into our feelings and just let them be that we can heal.

He was grateful to have even a few days of relief. Embracing all his feelings, even the fact that he missed his partner helped him gain more self-acceptance.

Gaining insight and perspective helped him to heal. He started to truly understand what he missed and realize what he truly needs in a relationship. He saw that the press of such needs helped propel him into this relationship even though a part of him always knew it wasn't good for him. He began to question whether it was love or attachment that kept him stuck in the first place.

Naturally, it was an up and down path towards healing but the better times grew in frequency and number and he was eventually able to feel happy with another.

This story has a very happy ending. Years later, I received a letter from him as well as a phone call thanking me. He met another woman who was very different from those in the past. They fell in love, married, and had a baby together. He became very happy.

2. Katrina

"I still go to the kitchen and look out the window. I am in love with a ghost. A ghost that can never be there for me."

Katrina was a talented, successful woman with a warm, engaging personality. She had a long history of relationships with men who were abusive or rejecting. This pattern was set up in childhood by her absent father and unsupportive mother.

When she first came to me, she was involved with a married man with whom she had a baby. He would often spend part of an evening with her but would be gone by morning. She would pine for him, especially in the morning.

Many a morning she would go to the kitchen window to see if his car was there. When he was not there, she would await his phone call.

"When he calls in the morning, I feel so alive…at what point did I lose myself to such an extent?"

One early morning they got up and he said he needed to leave. She went to the bathroom and when she came out, he was gone. She ran out to the street, pounded on his car door but he drove off. She was devastated. "How can he just leave me standing there in the cold? I felt shattered, like I'm falling apart."

We discussed how the breakup of a relationship is so disorganizing and she grabbed onto this notion saying it totally expressed her reality.

During a subsequent session she said, "I need to focus on why I keep doing this to myself over and over again instead of focusing on him."

I said that it is very hard to let go of an attachment and described how a person can get attached and view the other as their lifeline. She reflected on this and kept saying "attachment" over and over again.

The next session, she said she had done a lot of thinking about her relationship and how I used the word "attachment" not love to describe it. She said the word that came to mind was "parasite."

"Is it really him that I want or an attachment? And if it is really the attachment, then why am I so willing to be attached to just anything?"

One day she said, "I finally realized he isn't the man for me... Well, do I really love him, or the idea of love, the promise of not being alone, the hope of being together with someone. If that's the case, then I am a parasite looking to latch on to a life source to fulfill my unmet needs. I just happen to choose men that cannot or have no desire to meet me halfway. So I remain rejected, abandoned and alone. I do more than I have to do and sacrifice myself and my family to hold onto a ghost. Why can't I face myself? Why can't I be happy with myself? I have reinvented myself so outwardly. I am a confident, successful woman. But I don't believe it. And somehow I form attachments with people who reinforce what I truly believe about myself. Not good enough, will never measure up and it's only a matter of time before everyone finds out I am a fraud."

After describing her abusive, rejecting family of origin, she said, "I started to look outside for happiness, for acceptance and to feel worthy. Every relationship I have had has been based on my desperation, neediness, fear of abandonment and isolation. Everyone has ended the exact same way. I find these men who are not worthy of me and then I idolize them, and then somewhere along the way, I feel I can't live without them. I get into this parasitic mode and then the madness starts."

"Lost, paralyzed, abandoned, alone wandering in the wilderness with no particular direction. Knowing that I have been here before and understanding that I cannot be here again but not knowing how to not be here. I start my day alone again, another day without him by my side. I periodically go to the kitchen and look out the window to see if he has parked outside. He hasn't. The letdown, the incredible disappointment. How could he not be by my side, how could he be so detached from me? How could he not love me the way I love him, need him, crave him, yearn for him? I understand he can never be the man that I need to fulfill my needs. I understand that he can never be there for me 100%. I understand that love is sporadic. So given the fact that I understand all of that, why? Why do I run the gamut of emotions?"

Later, she said, "Am I feeding this relationship by focusing on it?"

She took a trip to Jamaica with this man and said it was wonderful the whole time, that he was totally there for her, causing her to doubt her decision to part. She said that within one day of her return, he went back to his old self, abandoning and abusing her as usual. She said she knows she has to accept the fact that he will never change. She then told me about her writings and I encouraged her to bring them in. We discussed how she has tremendous awareness but finds it so difficult to listen to her mind, not her heart. We discussed the concept of automatic thoughts and responses, we explored her history and how this has laid the groundwork for her current relationship. We explored the terrible void she experiences when he leaves, the panic and desperation. She is aware that she has terrible abandonment issues. The goal was to set limits and draw on her many strengths. I told her to turn to those things that are self-enhancing such as her creativity in her work.

She said she feels humiliated, ashamed and like an empty shell. I said that she needs to embrace all parts of herself, the fragility, the sadness, etc. She said, "I'm this whining, weak, shell of a person." I tried to reframe this saying she is emotional, passionate, in touch with her feelings, that she has a big heart, that these are good things, that she is truly alive whereas he is emotionally dead. I said, "I'd rather be you than him." This made an impact. I also said that this is a state, that it is temporary, it is by no means her whole reality or the future.

Katrina illustrates so many of the points outlined in this book and thus I have chosen her to integrate all the main points.

First, there is the description of the terrible pain she feels every time he leaves. Like Pat who was described in Part One, she used the word "shattered." This is a traumatic state and also shows how the breakup of a relationship can be such a disorganizing event.

The words "when he calls in the morning, I feel so alive. At what point did I lose myself to such an extent" describe why we stay in these relationships despite the handwriting on the wall. As I said, there is no greater high than falling in love and when we feel it slipping away we struggle to hold onto it. The death of love and the death of hope are terrible states and we will do anything to avoid them.

This statement also reflects not only the blow to herself but the way in which we can lose ourselves in a relationship. As I said in Part Two, we do lose a part of ourselves in a relationship and that is part of the price of intimacy. You become a part of each other and that is natural. However, in the case of Katrina, this man became her whole world and she totally lost herself in the relationship.

The statement "lost, paralyzed, abandoned, alone, wandering in the wilderness" eloquently describes the extent to which she lost herself in this relationship and struggled to regain her own self.

Her awareness that she is repeating history is reflected in her statement, "I need to be focusing on why I keep doing this to myself over and over again instead of focusing on him." She has a long history of abandonment beginning in childhood.

"I finally realized he isn't the man for me... Well, do I really love him, or the idea of love, the promise of not being alone, the hope of being together with someone."

She was hooked, not just on hope but on fantasy. The word "promise" conveys the hope as well as her description of how she pined for him every time he left. The words "idea of him" reveals how she was hooked on the fantasy of him, of what it might be like. Her description of him as a ghost for which she yearns also illustrates the extent of her fantasy. The fact that she could not extricate herself in spite of her awareness shows the extent to which she was hooked.

The role of intermittent reinforcement which I have described earlier contributes to being hooked in this way. Katrina described how, when they took a trip to Jamaica, he was there for her the whole time, causing her to doubt her decision to leave. Half the time he was not there for her but when he was, as he was during the trip to Jamaica, she received the type of reinforcement needed to keep her hooked on him and the fantasy of him.

She knew that attachment and longing are not love but could not help herself.

She used the words "needy, desperate, not good enough, will never measure up, and parasite" to describe herself and her attachment. Instead of seeing herself as a needy, desperate parasite, she needed to see herself as wanting and needing a lot. Self statements such as, "I want a lot, love a lot and need a lot" helped to reframe her feelings. Indeed, the notion of needing to embrace all parts of one's self in order to heal was exemplified as she described how she feels humiliated, ashamed and like an empty shell. She went on to say, "I'm this whining, weak, shell of a person." I tried to reframe this by saying she is emotional, passionate, in touch with her feelings, that she has a big heart, that she is truly alive and these are good things.

In reframing her feelings as such, I had hoped she would embrace all parts of herself including her fragility and sadness.

At some point, she said, "Am I feeding this relationship by focusing on it?" This is an excellent question. It is true that focusing on something serves to strengthen it. This is all part of an obsessional thought train which is self feeding.

Katrina had a great deal of self-awareness. She knew her own fragility, as well as the role of her past in feeding such a dysfunctional relationship. She was aware of her own fragilities and neediness that kept her stuck. She knew she was hooked on a fantasy and hope that could never be fulfilled.

Yet, she had a very difficult time extricating herself from this nightmare. She would free herself for a time but then get sucked in by false promises during moments of weakness.

She was tormented by the fact that, despite her awareness, she would remain stuck. This is a common complaint of many in therapy. They know themselves in and out but can't change. As she said, after describing how she knows he is not the man for her and is very bad for her, "Knowing this, why do I run the gamut of emotions?"

Awareness often doesn't seem to help, at least in the short run because it comes from an intellectual place and the heart does not listen to reason, it listens to feelings. I often say, "Listen to your gut, your inner voice; it never leads you wrong."

When Katrina started to listen to her inner voice and focus on herself and her many strengths, channeling her energy into her career and her baby, she was able to slowly but surely move on. As she put it, "I need to focus on why I keep doing this to myself over and over again instead of focusing on him."

Life for Katrina was a roller coaster for some time but she was committed to a vision of a happier life. She did not want to stay stuck in the past and nurturing a vision of a happier future guided her in years to come.

Conclusion

I want to thank my clients who have trusted me with their personal stories of terrible heartbreak. I have learned so much from all of you and even though my role is to help you, know that you have helped me as well and for that I am forever grateful.

Even though I know that one doesn't just get over a broken heart, it is my hope that this book will provide some sort of comfort, whether it be information, validation or the knowledge that you are not alone.

Whatever it is, my hope is that it will help someone with a broken heart to take the first steps towards the amazing journey of healing.

About the Author

Dr. June Owen is a clinical psychologist who has been in private practice for more than thirty years. She has extensive experience working with trauma, disability and loss. Her own personal traumatic losses have been an inspiration for this book. She is also a musician who has a passionate love of Nature as well as reading and creative writing and derives much sustenance from these things.

www.ingramcontent.com/pod-product-compliance
Lightning Source LLC
Chambersburg PA
CBHW031131020426
42333CB00012B/328